Did You Know Publishing, Inc.

presents...

ROSA PARKS

Prereaders/Early Readers

Dedication

To Jeanette, my wife, my advisor and my accountant;
to my daughter, Amber, and my son, William II;
to the entire Did You Know Publishing team who
shared with me information, time, and patience.
And to children and adults all over the world who have
been waiting this opportunity.

Published by *Did You Know Publishing, Inc.*
P.O. Box 157233
Cincinnati, Ohio 45215–7233

Library of Congress Catalog Card Number: 92–71756

ISBN: 0–9633151–0–2

Printed in the United States of America

10 9 8 7 6 5 4 3 2 1

Preface

The purpose of our publication is to introduce prereaders and early readers to African American contributions in American History. In most cases, these people and events have made major contributions and have gone relatively unknown. These historical events are presented in a colorful picturesque storybook fashion to capture the attention and to spark the imagination of children.

Note to the Parent/Teacher:

We the writers have purposely put some challenging words in our book; it is only by discovering new words that a child increases his or her vocabulary. So, for that reason, you will find a glossary with a brief definition in the back of our book. We hope you and your child/student will find our publication fun, enjoyable, and educational.

SPECIAL ACKNOWLEDGMENT TO SUPPORTING COMPANY

Caring Program for Children

This program provides health care benefits to needy children.

You can help. See Specially marked boxes of Crest for details.

SPONSORED BY

Crest.

*Known in California as CaliforniaKids. In Michigan, Crest makes a direct donation. No purchase or certificate mail–in is necessary

Printing made possible by
Crest Toothpaste
and
Procter & Gamble Educational Services

This is a story about a **historical** bus ride taken by Rosa Parks.

1

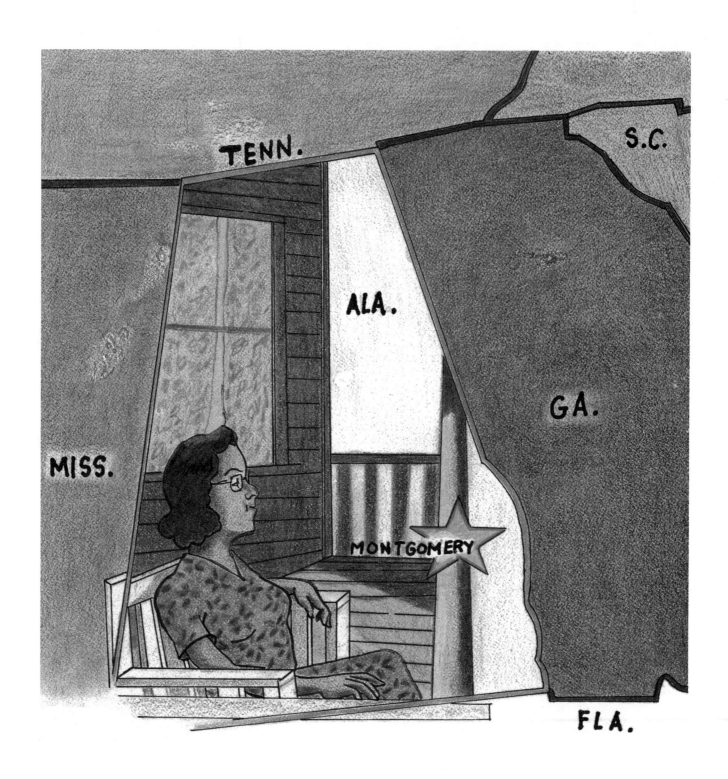

Rosa Parks lived in Montgomery, Alabama.

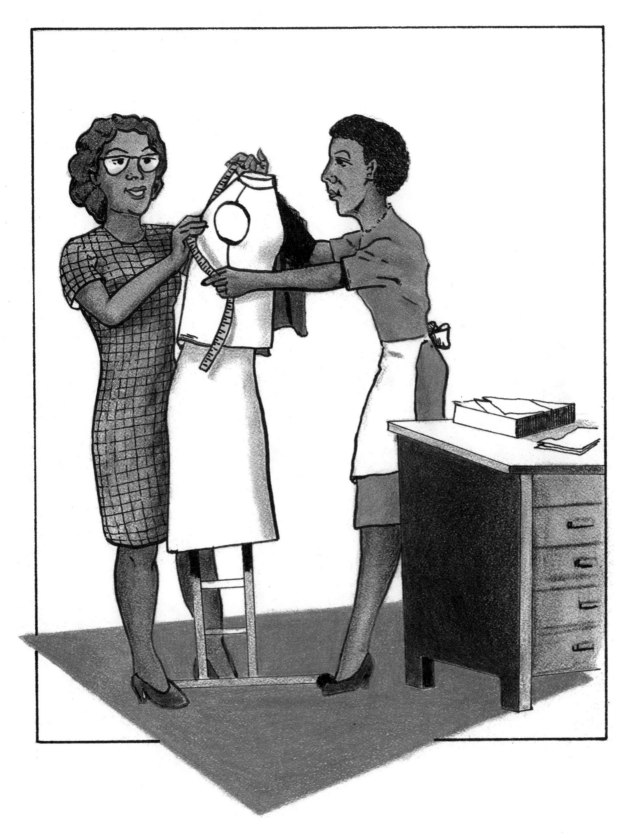

She was a **seamstress** at a tailor shop. Ms. Parks loved her work and was good at making clothes.

On December 1, 1955, Ms. Parks decided to do some shopping downtown.

She shopped at several stores.

After a while, Ms. Parks became very
tired and her feet began to hurt.

She decided to ride the bus home.

Ms. Parks boarded the bus and paid her fare to the bus driver. She took a seat near the front of the bus.

On the bus were black people and white people.

In those days blacks were separated from whites. Blacks and whites could not sit together on the bus. This separation is known as **segregation**.

The bus stopped to pick up more people.
Some were white and some were black.

Some people had to stand because
the bus was overcrowded.

The bus driver noticed a white person
standing while Ms. Parks was sitting
near the front of the bus.

To let the white person sit down, the
bus driver ordered Ms. Parks to give up
her seat and go to the back of the bus.

Ms. Parks would not move.

Because she refused to give up her seat, Ms.
Parks was arrested by the police and put in jail.
After a short period of time, Ms. Parks was
released from jail.

However, many people became very angry about
what happened to Ms. Parks. They felt that
segregation on the bus lines was unfair.

They believed that people should be
able to sit anywhere on a bus.

Many people of Montgomery, Alabama, joined together and decided to boycott the bus lines.

The **boycott** ended **segregation** on the city
buses. Today people can sit anywhere they
choose on a bus.

Ralph
Abernathy

Rosa Parks

Dr. Martin Luther King Jr.

Because of her courage to do what was right,
Rosa Parks is often referred to as the mother
of the **civil rights movement**.

Many people live in the United States of America.

Some are African American, some are Caucasian, some are American Indian, some are Hispanic, and some are Asian.

All these people are important and make
America great. Rosa Parks proved to us
that everyone should be treated the same.

Glossary

(A) Boycott   To join together in refusing to go along with something that you feel is not fair (see pages 19 and 20).

(B) Civil Rights   The rights promised to all people that they must be treated fair and equal (see page 21).

(C) Historical   Based on people or events of the past (see page 1).

(D) Movement   Organization of people working toward the same thing (see page 21).

(E) Seamstress   A woman who has a job sewing (see page 3).

(F) Segregation   A law that would separate you from others based on your skin color (see pages 10, 17 and 20).

Ralph
Abernathy

Rosa Parks

Dr. Martin Luther King Jr.